Battleship Yamato

Of war, beauty and irony

Battleship Yamato

Of war, beauty and irony

Jan Morris

LIVERIGHT PUBLISHING CORPORATION
A Division of W.W. Norton & Company
Independent Publishers Since 1923
New York London

The hero
Coxinga faces a
tiger, *Kuniyoshi,
c. 1842*

Contents

Explanatory

This little work is a sort of illustrated reverie, a literary meditation inspired by the story of the Japanese battleship Yamato. *In her day she was the most powerful warship in the world, and she* was sunk in a suicide mission during the American assault on Okinawa in the very last months of the Second World War.

In reading her story I have been struck by its figurative aspects. It has seemed to me to express all the varied emotions evoked by that ultimate public catastrophe, war, and not least by irony, its inescapable concomitant. For while war is always misery, it has not always been misery unalloyed. Down the centuries, men (if more seldom women) have paradoxically drawn inspiration of many kinds from the experiences of conflict, and I have found many of them expressed in the story of Yamato: *I mean the pride and splendour of it all, the undeniable beauty, the excitement of battle, the elegiac calm of defeat, the magnificence of human strength and courage, and through it all the bitter power of irony, tempering the squalor, the carnage and the degradation.*

Such is my subject.

Before we start, I should tell you about the ship. On my desk in Wales stand models of three battleships (as a particular class of warship, that is). I keep them there in historical allegory. Each ship flies the flag of a different nation, and represents a final interpretation of the battleship as a weapon, but in trilogy they emblemize for me the extinction of the imperialist ideology, the right of one community to lord it over another. For generations the battleship was a prime executor of this notion, and in my mind those small models stand there beyond my computer as symbols of the end of Empire, which has been in one way or another an obsession of my own life and calling.

All three battleships were launched in the 1940s, during the Far Eastern war, and they were the last word in warships, the latest in the long line of capital ships that had been for so long the measure of national power. Prince of Wales, *35,000 tons, was built on the River Clyde.* Bismarck, *43,000 tons, was built on the Elbe.* Yamato, *56,000 tons, was built at Kure, on the Inner Sea of Japan. In themselves they were properly representative, as it later turned out, of their respective nations.*

The British Royal Navy had been for generations the very criterion of sea-power, and the true engine of the world-wide empire that the British ruled. Since the beginning of the twentieth century it had also been, the pace-maker of naval architecture and technique — the name of the revolutionary British battleship Dreadnought, launched in 1910, had gone into the dictionaries to to signify the entire breed of capital ships. However by the 1940s the Royal Navy's supremacy was much weakened. International treaties had limited its power, financial stringencies had inhibited its shipbuilding, and Prince of Wales was no Dreadnought. In particular her main armament of 14-inch guns was less than formidable, and Winston Churchill himself mourned her weakness.

HMS Prince of Wales in 1941

The Imperial German Navy was by comparison an upstart, and in fact had come into being in direct response to British naval supremacy. Its real creator was the Kaiser, Wilhelm II, who inspired the creation of a formidable German fleet to rival the British in the First World War. Technically advanced, especially in submarine warfare, it had held its own in the one great sea battle of that conflict, at Jutland in 1916, and when the Second World War broke out Adolf Hitler saw it as a vital strategic asset. Bismarck *was in every respect the very latest*

Bismarck *in 1940*

thing, just as Nazism was projected as the ultimate ideology, and her main armament was of 15-inch guns.

And finally there was Yamato, *the biggest, heaviest and most powerful of the three. She had a slightly smaller sister ship, but* Musashi *was never to achieve the iconic, almost ritual magnetism of* Yamato – *the ultimate battleship, the pride of the Imperial Japanese Navy. The IJN itself was animated by a heady mixture of Nelsonian example – it was modelled upon the British navy – and a native mysticism of immense martial potency. In 1945* Yamato *herself was also the ultimate expression of Japanese imperialism – of imperialism itself, one might say. She was the Dreadnought of Dreadnoughts. Her main armament was of 18.1-inch guns, and she was legendary in her own lifetime.*

This is the ship, then, that has inspired my reverie, or meditation. Let us see where she lies.

Overleaf: Yamato *performing full power trials, 1941*

Prologue

On a day in early April 1945 *Yamato* is at anchor with nine escort vessels, a light cruiser and eight destroyers, off the village of Mitajiri in the Inland Sea of Japan. They constitute the Second Fleet of the Imperial Japanese Navy. The roadstead is near the southern extremities of the Japanese archipelago, and we may imagine an almost lyrical scene there. Low wooded hills shelter the anchorage. To the east are the waters of the Inland Sea, to the south the fierce mysteries of the Sea of Japan, where the Ryukyu islands are, and beyond them the far-scattered isles and atolls of the South Pacific. It is a prospect, as I see it from the next century with my alien European eye, allegorically Japanese, instinct with the traditions of a proud, ancient and warlike culture; and it is to honour those traditions that the three thousand-odd sailors on board *Yamato* are awaiting the command to go into battle against the Americans.

What millions of fighting men, down the centuries, have waited for battle before them all over the world! It is one of the classic

Opposite: Yamato *(bottom) at anchor, 1942 or 1943*

recurring moments of history and of art — warriors and their weapons at peace, but ready for imminent war. Generally there is cheerful defiance or merriment to those moments, but often of course it is, as the English used to say, Dutch courage. It was always so. Homer says that when Agamemnon and his princes prepared themselves for war against the Trojans, they feasted upon a sacrificial bull, roasted with livers and kidneys, and they ate, he says, "as much as they could swallow." The Trojans, on the other hand, in different martial mood, sat around campfires among their tethered chariots, munching pearl-barley mixed with wheat, and "awaiting the regal glory of dawn."

Achilles and Ajax playing chess before battle

On the very eve of Waterloo the *crème de la crème* of the English armies danced the night away in Brussels — as Thackeray's Becky says, "there was everybody there that everybody knew, and only a very few nobodies in the whole ballroom." After the first day's fighting at Gettysburg in 1862, Confederate soldiers awaiting the next day's slaughter

RAF pilots waiting to be called into action, 1940

found themselves unexpectedly cheered by the arrival of a visiting military band. Aristocratic German night-fighter pilots, in the 1940s, waited in their dinner-jackets for the call to defend Berlin against British bombers, while on the other side the young bravos of the Battle of Britain, so delightfully boyish if we are to believe the old movies, roistered at their mess-tables before their call to kill or be killed.

But Montaigne tells us that before Spartan warriors went into battle they made sacrifices to the Muses, praying that their deeds be well and worthily written about.

★ ★ ★

So it goes. I think myself, though, that there is a more ambiguous, more profound suggestiveness to the presence at such a time of ships of war waiting for action. There is poetry already to *their* images. Of all the historians' epithets I know, the one that stirs me most is Admiral Mahan's characterization of eighteenth-century blockading warships in the Napoleonic wars – "those far-distant, storm-tossed ships, upon which the Grand Army never looked, that stood between it and the dominion of the world" – unless it be Winston Churchill's vision of the British battlefleet, moving to its war stations at Scapa Flow in 1914 "like giants bowed in anxious thought."

And who can deny an allure to the grim silhouette of the German battleship *Tirpitz*, in the Norwegian Altafjord in the cruel 1940s – snowy mountains all around, waters black and silent, the strangely camouflaged man-of-war lurking there in prologue, as it were, ready to fall when the time came upon her victims out at sea? Vicious, cruel, but beautiful in its kind, like a tiger on a leash.

Previous pages: Leonidas and the Spartans before the battle of Thermopylae, (detail), by Jacques-Louis David, 1814

Opposite: Tirpitz *in the Altafjord, winter 1943*

Tiger on a Leash

Such a waiting ship, at such a time, at such a haven, is *Yamato* that April day. As I watch her there in my imagination I seem to sense a sort of tremulous serenity to her presence, motionless among her escorts off the Mitajiri shore. No other ships come by. To the south, where the Bungo Strait reaches the open sea, all is threat and foreboding: here, in this sheltered roadstead among the hills of home, *Yamato* lies waiting. For one of my sensibility she is more than a mere ship, more than a machine, more even than a weapon, but an amalgam of universal human emotions.

Her style, though, is overwhelmingly Japanese. Her silhouette is long, low and threatening, like something in a tapestry. Her lines are elegantly rakish. Amidships, her complex control tower looks futuristic, and her solitary funnel is heavily raked, almost as if she is perpetually sailing against a hurricane. Discreetly unobtrusive, as though they are lying low, are the three huge turrets of her main guns, two forward of the tower, one aft, and she is painted a muted silver-grey.

Opposite: Yamato *at the Truk anchorage, Caroline Islands, where she spent most of 1943*

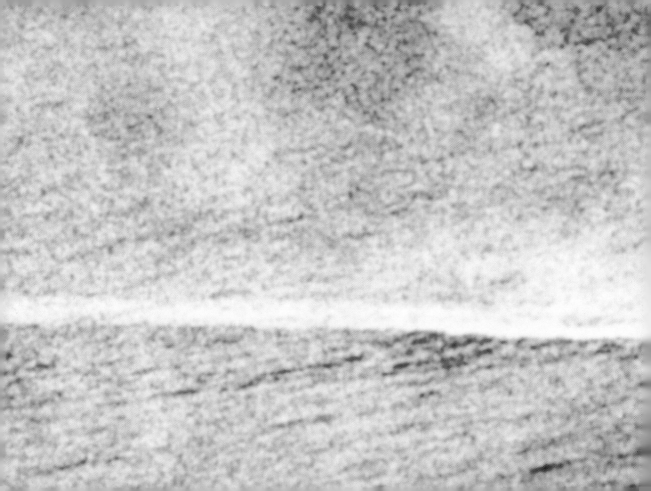

Even her enemies think her a beautiful ship, and to me she possesses beauty of an allegorical kind, too, a beauty of suggestion. Chopin might have orchestrated it, with his streaks of something dark among the ecstasies, and aboard *Yamato* those three thousand Japanese men, most of them young, are living it themselves. This is because *Yamato* is no ordinary battleship, but the most powerful warship there has ever been. To be manning this greatest of war-vessels, to be serving their country in the most magnificent of all its instruments of power – for the seamen aboard *Yamato* it is honour unparalleled. At the prow of the ship is the chrysanthemum crest, in gold, that has been for five centuries the symbol of Japanese imperial glory, and the very name of the vessel is an ancient poetical eponym for Japan itself.

Yamato *(or* Musashi*), with the chrysanthemum crest just visible on a ship in the foreground, 1943*

Previous pages: Yamato *in action during the Battle off Samar, October 25, 1944*

Opposite: Few photographs survive from on board Yamato, *but her layout was almost identical to* Musashi, *seen here on the occasion of a visit by the Emperor Hirohito and staff in 1943*

So *Yamato* waits, but not with roast beef and kidneys, not with ball-room preening or dinner at the Hotel Adlon, but possibly with a prayer or two to the Muses. All seems calm out there, and when night falls all is dark too, except for the occasional blinking of a signal lamp between *Yamato* and the light cruiser *Yahagi*, the leader of her support squadron. Tomorrow, perhaps, the battleship will have its sailing orders, not from an Agamemnon or an Adolf Hitler, but ultimately from the divinely incarnate Emperor Hirohito of Japan, 124th in the legendary line of succession from the sun-goddess Amaterasu.

Opposite: The Emperor Hirohito (facing camera) inspecting installations on the bridge of Musashi, *1943. This may be the only surviving image of this area of either battleship*

Line of Succession

Let us stand back for a moment from our imaginary watch-post above the Mitajiri roadstead, store our binoculars and consider the historic reasons for *Yamato*'s presence there.

It is almost the end of the Pacific War, essentially between the Japanese monarchy (population 124 million) and the USA (population 255 million), but forming one vast element of the ideological conflict that has engaged half the world since 1939. It began four years ago when the Japanese, in a crazed revival of their immemorial militarism, for no sane reason attacked from the air the United States Pacific Fleet, at anchor in its home port of Pearl Harbor, Hawaii. At a blow they disabled most of it. Almost at the same time they seized Hong Kong and Singapore from the colonial British, the East Indies from the Dutch, and so for the brutal moment made themselves omnipotent in the eastern seas. From the China coast to the approaches to Australia, from the Aleutians to the Solomon Islands, Japanese fleets and armies ruled the Pacific Ocean.

Opposite: Yamato *narrowly avoids being hit on retreat from the Battle of the Sibuyan Sea, October 26, 1944*

Times have changed since then, though. The colossal strength of the USA, at sea, in the air, in its factories, its bank accounts, its board-rooms and its universities, has been assembled to drive the Japanese step by step from their island territories and conquests. The grotesque Japanese bluff was called almost from the start. At Guadalcanal, Guam and Iwo Jima American amphibious forces have won bitter campaigns: at Midway American fleets and aircraft have triumphed in the most decisive sea-battle in the history of warfare. By now the Americans are at the gates of Japan itself, and ready to attack its ultimate outpost in the Pacific Ocean, the island of Okinawa. They have already bombed Tokyo itself, and up their sleeve, so to speak, is the ultimate war-winning weapon, the nuclear bomb. Only Okinawa awaits them first.

★ ★ ★

For the moment *Yamato*'s own intentions are unknown to her crew. Many of those three thousand seamen probably realize that their war is almost lost. Japan's last desperate technique of arms has been the profligate use of single-seat suicide aircraft, *kamikaze*, "divine wind," to throw themselves in sacrifice at individual American ships. Now *kamikaze* pilots and aircraft are running short, while the Japanese surface fleet has been decimated in desperate rearguard actions against overwhelming odds. The Second Fleet, ten ships in all, is almost all that is left afloat. What use the High Command in Tokyo will make of it, with *Yamato* a last magnificent arrow in the imperial quiver, the next few hours will reveal.

In the meantime her crew prepare themselves for the worst and the best, as fighting men have braced themselves since the invention of war, and next morning we ourselves, from our vantage points in space and time, may watch them through our virtual instruments. If the scene looks at first sight placid, that is misleading. Everything on *Yamato*, we soon realize, is in a condition of taut preparedness. Equipment is being checked, orders prepared, guns inspected, radars calibrated, signals exchanged, staffs briefed, drills rehearsed. There is a little thatched Shinto shrine on board the battleship, and there throughout the day men pause to bow and clap their hands in reverence.

And when somebody on watch in the control tower shouts "cherry blossom!", binoculars are raised all along the rail of the great ship to catch a glimpse of early April flowers on the shore – Japanese cherries, Japanese souls, messengers of spring and very emblems of Japanese naval honour and mystic sacrifice.

If only one might fall
(as a contemporary *haiku* had it)
Like cherry blossoms in the spring –
So pure and radiant . . .

In the afternoon a cutter comes alongside with fifty young cadets fresh from the Imperial Naval Academy on the island of Etajima. They have just graduated after four years of intensive training in all that it means to be a Japanese naval officer, physically, academically, ideologically and not least psychologically. The idea of sacrificial duty, pure and radiant, is ingrained in them, together with the conviction that battles can be won by single deadly blows, *samurai* style.

Opposite: Sailors relaxing on the deck of Yamato*'s sister ship,* Musashi*, 1942. The foredeck, later filled with anti-aircraft defences, was identical to that of* Yamato

So they are thrilled by the prospect of imminent action, overwhelm-ingly proud of the distinction of service on the ultimate battleship; but as they hasten up the gangplank, so spick, span and eager, we may guess they are watched with mordant humour by hardened old salts from the deck above. Humour of one kind or another has always brought its own sort of prophylactic to the menaces of war. Soldiers, sailors and airmen of all nationalities, all ages, have laughed or sung their way to conflict, and not always bitterly. Even in our own time fighting men have actually enjoyed themselves – how often have we heard thoroughly decent elderly gentle-men confess that their happiest days were the days of their wars, the days of their youth, the days that brought out the best in them? "I adore war," the English poet Julian Grenfell wrote to his mother before he was killed in action in 1916. "One loves one's fellow-man so much more when one is bent on killing him."

So among the old hands of *Yamato*, too, joking among themselves as they watch those rosy-cheeked youths come aboard, black pre-battle humour surely prevails; and as the day passes, and it becomes known that

Opposite: Cadets aboard
Yamato, March 1945

Yamato will be sailing into action the very next morning, so a kind of official festivity is ordered, too. Just for an hour or two the iron discipline of the service is deliberately relaxed. Junior officers are given cigarettes as presents from the emperor himself. Rice wine is distributed among all ranks. Sounds of celebration reach us across the darkening water, and we can see through our hypothetical lenses that around the decks there is a suggestion of bacchanalia. Glasses are being splintered, songs hazily sung, and we can glimpse sailors tipsily dancing among the massive gun turrets.

It is an ordered bacchanalia, though, down there across the water, and after an hour or two the command comes over the loudspeakers that the good times must end. Tradition has been honoured, and before nightfall order is restored. The fifty young cadets, to their chagrin, are sent ashore after all, and stand tearfully to the salute as their picket-boat withdraws. A few older and sick seamen go with them, and at midnight two destroyers arrive, and mooring themselves one to the starboard side of *Yamato*, one to the port, refuel the battleship for the next day's war.

Opposite: Promotion ceremony aboard Yamato, *March 1945*

Overleaf: Blossoming Cherry Trees, *by Sakai Hoitsu, 1805*

For the Next Day's War

Yamato's enemies are aware that she is there. High-flying American aircraft have repeatedly flown over Mitajiri, and American submarines are doubtless prowling in wait around the channels from the Inland Sea to the Pacific. A week ago amphibious forces of the US Pacific Command landed in immense strength on Okinawa, and the Japanese have already responded with a nightmarish *kamikaze* assault upon them: but the Americans can have no doubt that *Yamato* herself is destined to play a part in the ultimate battle for the island, sure to be the very last great battle of the Pacific war.

In many ways the ship is still a mystery to them. Her sister ship *Musashi* they sank from the air four months before, but without giving them a chance to inspect her, and *Yamato* herself had been built in extreme secrecy in a purpose-built dry dock at Kure in the Inland Sea. Throughout her construction the dock was screened for security by huge bamboo mats and nets of sisal, and strangers of every kind were

Opposite: Possibly the only photograph of Yamato *being built, taken on September 20, 1941. This is a view from the stern, with one of the barrels of the after 18-inch gun at maximum elevation. The ship on the right is* Hosho, *the world's first purpose-built aircraft carrier*

kept away. American intelligence knew little about the details of the ship: Japanese counter-intelligence had put about deceptions concerning its size and in particular the size of its guns. We now know that *Yamato* far exceeded the size agreed by pre-war international treaties, and carried the biggest guns and the heaviest armour of any warship afloat. The main turrets alone were so heavy – each as heavy as a destroyer – that lesser vessels had to be constructed just to convey them from factory to shipyard. *Yamato*'s main armament was the most powerful on any ship anywhere, and she also had at least 150 smaller guns and carried seven reconnaissance seaplanes. What the *Tirpitz* was to British naval planners of the day, *Yamato* was to the American High Command in the Pacific – a very present danger, or in herself, as the old strategists used to say, "A fleet in being."

And as for the Japanese High Command, she was to its admirals, as she is to me, not just a formidable statistic, but a symbol and an epitome. That model of her is before me as I write, picked up years ago at a charity shop in Wales, and in the glow from my computer screen her silhouette

Opposite: One of the three colossal 18.1-inch gun turrets of Yamato *being assembled*

still strikes me as lovely, dreadful, pitiful and reproachful – sad components of beauty, don't you think?

★ ★ ★

Reproachful? In a way, because the very notion of the battleship as a history-defining weapon of war has already been discredited – and by the Japanese themselves. The men of the *Yamato* are well aware that two of the most powerful British capital ships, *Prince of Wales* and *Repulse*, were ignominiously sunk by Japanese torpedo bombers four years ago: and they know too that the American victories in the Pacific have been gained above all by vast numbers of aircraft operating from aircraft carriers. By 1945 big warships operating without air cover are hopelessly vulnerable to air attack, and *Yamato* has none – five of her seaplanes have been disembarked as unsuitable for battle, leaving only one slow reconnaissance aircraft on board. A bitter Navy joke had it that history knew of three supreme follies – the Great Wall of China, the Pyramids and IJN *Yamato*… So perhaps there is an element of resentment to the responses of her crew,

Opposite: Yamato *manoeuvering to avoid aerial attack, October 24, 1944. The shadow of an American plane can be seen*

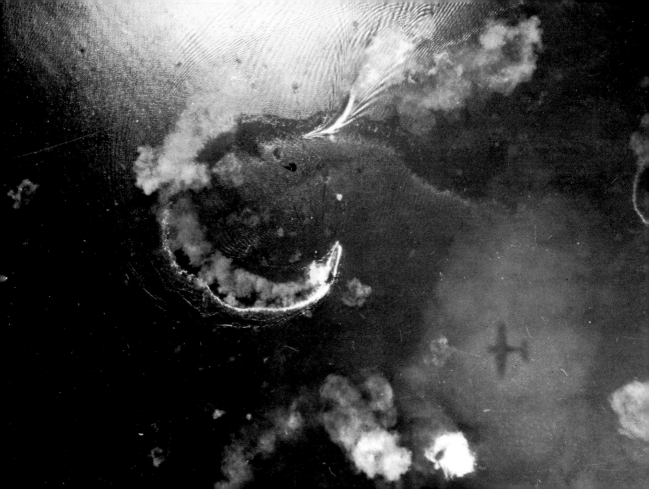

however fervent their patriotism, when on the morning of April 5 they are mustered on deck to be told the purpose of their presence.

Rear-Admiral Ariga Kosaku

We can hear the order over the ship's loud-hailers, and the clatter of a thousand boots as the men double to their stations in the foredeck. We can perhaps see Rear Admiral Ariga Kosaku, captain of *Yamato,* clambering to the top of the forward turret, and if only in mental echo hear what is he telling the serried mass of men in the deck below him. He talks to them as friends and fellow-countrymen, with a message from the commander-in-chief of the Imperial Japanese Navy. *Yamato* and her escorts are to constitute a Special Attack Force, and are to make an immediate sortie code-named Operation Ten-ichi-go (Operation Heaven Number One) – which some interpreted as meaning a heaven-sent opportunity to reverse bad luck . . .

Opposite:
Anti-aircraft gunners
aboard Yamato, *1945*

The little force, without its own air cover, is to hurl itself out of the Inner Sea to fall upon the United States forces attacking Okinawa, in coordination with an aerial assault by the remaining *kamikaze* pilots. It would fight to the death, as the High Command message portentously puts it, to "destroy the enemy fleet completely, and establish an eternal foundation for the Japanese Empire."

★ ★ ★

Eternal foundation? Ha! Listen to the cheering now! All the esoterica of Japanese patriotism explodes. The war-cries of *Banzai – Ten Thousand Years!* The deep massed unison of *Kimigayo*, the national anthem, echoing across the bay! The ceremonial bows in the direction of the distant Emperor! Translated into my universal imagery, this really is a Shakespearean, Nelsonian, Napoleonic, Tennysonian moment – St Crispin's Day in the Inner Sea! Stiffen the sinews! Summon up the blood! History is watching! Every man will do his duty! On, on, you noble Japanese, into the jaws of death!

Opposite: Warrant officers photographed aboard Yamato, *January 1945*

For yes, it is not only we, a century on, who know the fate of Ten-ichi-go. The sailors might cheer their captain, but all too many of them, we may be sure, understand what that message means. *Yamato* herself is to commit suicide, as the noblest of *kamikaze* weapons. At best she is to beach herself on an Okinawan coral and in her death-throes use all her guns, all her ammunition, all her heroes, in support of the Japanese army. At worst, she is simply to blast away at her enemies until she herself is sunk. Either way, she will act as a terrific decoy, to divert American attention from the frenzied last assaults of the *kamikaze* pilots.

The Americans, we know now, have fallen upon Okinawa with 1,500 ships and 250,000 men, and they have thousands of attack aircraft on call. There is not a hope in hell for *Yamato,* her nine consorts and her patriots of the Second Fleet, except the wan and glorious hope of sacrifice.

Among those who realize all this is Admiral Ariga himself, the

Opposite: Flight deck on USS Yorktown, *winter 1943. The planes include Hellcats and Avengers. The ship later took part in the sinking of* Yamato

battleship's captain. He recognizes the tragic folly of the Ten-ichi-go sortie. So does the commander of the whole task force, and the commander of the escort squadron, and many of the men who summoned the blood and shouted *banzai* at their own Harfleur or Crimea that day.

    Yamato and her consorts prepare to sail at 1500 hours on April 6, but before they weigh anchor we watchers from the shore see a solitary biplane seaplane fly in from the north, and alight splashily beside the battleship. It carries Admiral Ryunosuke Kusaka, chief of staff of the Japanese Combined Fleet, and he has flown down from fleet headquarters near Tokyo to ensure that Ten-ichi-go goes ahead as planned by the High Command, whatever the reservations of its own captains. Actually he has profound doubts about the project himself; but after several hours of discussion on board *Yamato*, and agitated comings and goings among the support ships, we see his plane take off once more to salutes all round, and fly away into the afternoon. He has persuaded all the reluctant captains into the sortie, and thus he has himself, in person, decreed the fate of *Yamato*.

Admiral Ryunosuke Kusaka

He must know it. What does he feel, we wonder, as his plane disappears over the hills? He has marshalled destiny, and he doubtless feels the awful responsibility of power – and the awful beauty of it, too.

> *Upon the king! Let us our lives, our souls,*
> *Our debts, our careful wives,*
> *Our children and our sins lay on the king . . .*

Possibly Admiral Kusaka sees himself like Meissonier's celebrated Napoleon, grim-faced on a white horse, leading his marshals to defend the homeland in 1814. Or more probably he enacts in his mind some heroic bloody episode of Japanese historical legend, fitting to the occasion and worthy of himself – *Banzai, Kimigayo,* 10,000 years of glory . . .

Softly, anyway, as we watch and listen, the great engines thud, lines are cast away, signal lamps flash from ship to ship and *Yamato* sails tremendously into the dusk – away from the sweet waters of Japan, where the cherry-blossom flowers, towards her nemesis at 30°22′N, 128°04′E, halfway to Okinawa.

*...4 (detail),
...nier, 1864*

Halfway There

How are we to illustrate, or orchestrate, or evoke the presence of the Special Attack Force, as *Yamato* and her escorts get under way that evening, and pass through the Bungo Strait into the waters of the Pacific? Musically, Mendelssohn's Violin Concerto will be fine, with the young man's swing of it, the joy of action, the excitement of new waters, whether it be the Grand Canal or the Bungo Strait. In art I think of Emanuel Leutze's famous picture of General George Washington crossing the icy Delaware with his soldiers, during a Christmas coup of the American Revolution. You know the one – the huddled boatmen at their oars, the handsome hero bundled in his cloak, flags all tangled in the icy wind but the whole scene epically aflame with hope and challenge, even to the morning star that is guiding them to victory.

But for evocation we must, as Shakespeare had it, "on our imaginary forces work." It certainly looks a splendid little flotilla that we see entering the strait down there. At its centre sails of course *Yamato* herself, flying

Opposite: The IJN leaving anchorage for battle in the Philippines, October 22, 1944. Yamato *is third from right,* Musashi *second*

Overleaf: Washington crossing the Delaware *(detail), by Emanuel Leutze, 1851*

spectacularly at her main-mast the tremendous naval ensign of the rising sun, and the inscribed white banner that invokes the ancient fighting glories of the *samurai*. Now that we see her on the move at last she looks what she is – a monstrously elegant weapon of war, 71,000 tons of it, 863 feet long, more heavily armoured than any other ship afloat, which can sail at 27 knots and fire projectiles weighing nearly two tons to a distance of 26 miles at a rate of 7.5 per minute from each of its nine heaviest guns. Bringing up the rear is the cruiser *Yahagi*, 8,500 tons, and in formation on each flank are the eight destroyers, poetically named in the high Japanese style – "Shore Breeze", "Morning Frost", "Snow Wind", "Winter Moon"...

The two-ton "Beehive" shells designed for Yamato

Every one of those ships down there has been in battle before – even *Yamato* herself, which has served unobtrusively in two Pacific actions. All the destroyers have played their part in the fighting retreat, from one archipelago to another, one island and atoll to the next, across thousands of miles of ocean during the four years of the

Pacific war. Their performance has often been brilliant, as the Americans themselves have admitted, and they are nearly all modern ships. Lean, low in the water, hungry-looking, no wonder they have a cocky air. They know the odds against them, but no one has sunk them yet! As Captain Tameichi Hara of *Yahagi* has already written home to his family: "Be proud of me. Farewell!"

By now they have been spotted time and again by American reconnaissance planes, themselves keeping out of range of the warships' guns. Without a doubt American submarines are waiting for them in the Bungo Strait that must be their passage to the open sea, and Admiral Ariga realizes that his ship is presently to be at the heart of a great historic drama. He orders that an inspirational signal flag should be prepared – the Z flag. It was a legendary signal. The great Admiral Togo ordered it in 1905 when he led the IJN to victory against the Russians in the battle of Tsushima, a moment immortalized in art as in legend,

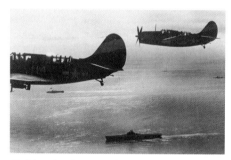

Helldiver bombers with ships of Task Force 58 on their way to Kyushu, March 1945

but its message came directly from the father of naval tradition, Nelson himself. "On this one battle," it said, "rests the destiny of our nation. Let every man do his utmost."

We know now that not so far away another fateful signal is being prepared. Two separate American fleets are waiting for *Yamato*, one chiefly of elderly battleships commanded by Admiral Raymond Spruance, the other chiefly of aircraft carriers commanded by the naval aviator Vice-Admiral Marc Mitscher. When the route of the Special Attack Force becomes clear, Mitscher asks Spruance which of their two forces should fall upon its ships, and the reply would also go into naval lore.

Admiral Spruance (left) and Vice-Admiral Mitscher

YOU TAKE THEM, Admiral Spruance simply signals.

★ ★ ★

But the Attack Force knows nothing of this, and sails resolutely on. The weather is drizzly, but presently the ships are sailing at 20 knots, battened down for action, regularly zig-zagging; the white streaks of its parallel wakes forming a moving pattern on the water, its funnel smokes a billowing cloud above. All in all it makes for a fine sight, a brave sight, as it leaves Japan for Okinawa.

For several hours, actually, Japan is still with it, on both sides of its passage. To the east is the big mainland island of Shikoku, to the west its counterpart Kyushu, and both are still in sight as they sail through the strait into enemy seas. Once a formation of Japanese Zero fighters flies over the fleet, but the only Japanese ships they sight are a little convoy of transports, shabby and despondent, plodding homeward from the battle zone. They exchange signals – "We pray for your success" – "We will not disappoint you" – but there are no sailors on the transports' decks to wave *Yamato* goodbye, or raise a cheer of *Banzai!*

As it is, when night falls and the moon comes up, *Yamato*'s men are on the lookout only for symptoms of submarines. Every man is at his battle-station, in battle-gear, in blacked-out quarters of the ship. We can envisage Ariga, humming to himself as was his habit, in his captain's station at the very summit of the control tower; and Vice-Admiral Ito, commander of the task force, silent in his command cabin on the bridge-deck, or perhaps snatching a thoughtful few moments at the nearby shrine; and the radar men unceasingly at their instruments in their dark enclave; and the damage control crews checking and re-checking their gear deep in the ship's hull; and the hundreds of off-duty seamen, all over *Yamato*, trying to get a few hours' sleep, or thoughtfully eating the ever-popular bean soup and dumplings that are the carefully chosen evening rations.

Vice-Admiral Seiichi Ito on Yamato, *January 1945*

And on the combat bridge are the twenty or so men who are navigating the Special Attack Force through those threatening seas. Even before they emerge from the Strait the radar men have reported the lurking presence of two American submarines, and from now on *Yamato* is, as it were, never at liberty. The mood on the battleship changes as the night draws on. Gone the carefree bravado, gone the Mendelssohnian melody, and all is grim concentration. Once out in the open sea there is a sudden change of route. Instead of proceeding due south to Okinawa, as the enemy probably expects, after midnight the task force turns to the west through the narrow Osumi Strait, to approach its targets from the other flank.

On the bridge only the shaded lights of instruments cast a dim glow, and the fluorescent dots on the caps of the senior officers move about like fireflies in the dark. Sporadic murmurs break the silence. Even at our conceptual distance we feel the quivering tension, and hear in our imagination some very different music – Sibelius or Mahler, don't you think, or something tremendously Wagnerian? The ship's lumbering seaplanes have been off-loaded, and the task force is totally without air cover. In gunpits and turrets all around the ship, though, in massed cluster around the control tower, thickly distributed on every deck, *Yamato*'s artillery is ready for anti-aircraft action: even the eleven vast 18-inch guns are primed to fire the anti-aircraft shells, nicknamed Beehive, that are designed to explode in mid-air and destroy entire enemy squadrons at a time. In short, *Yamato* is primed for Armageddon – and beyond.

Beyond Armageddon

To my mind the painter Picasso, as far away from the action as we are ourselves, foresaw it all. There was no ship to be sunk in his epochal masterpiece *Guernica,* which he had painted in 1937, and there were no horses with the Special Attack Force, but the essence and the meaning of *Yamato*'s coming ordeal are there in his artist's vision for us to see – whether in foresight, retrospection or imagination, for it is a vision beyond time, and while it ostensibly commemorates the useless horrors of the Spanish Civil War, as I see it its meanings are our own. For me *Guernica* is a scene of disillusionment, all greys, blacks and whites, no colour, no sound, fury signifying nothing. The tortured horse and the anguished bull in the picture have suffered to no purpose. The human beings are scarcely human. The lamp illuminates nothing. The whole scene seems to me to be groping, crying for meaning and finding none.

Previous pages and opposite:
Guernica, *by Pablo Picasso,*
1937

It is a picture of pandaemonium, and so I choose it to stand in illustration of *Yamato*'s final navigation: because the voyage towards Okinawa is going to take her, and us, not merely into Armageddon, the ultimate battle between good and evil, but into Chaos, where meanings are distorted, and values themselves seem meaningless.

★ ★ ★

Even beauty? Perhaps. *Yamato* met her destiny face to face on April 7, 1945, when she was still 200 miles from Okinawa, in open sea west of the Osumi-gunto islands. The day had opened sullenly, in mist and drizzle, and the scene was hushed – no aircraft in the sky, no ships in sight except *Yahagi* and the destroyers, still zig-zagging in fast formation alongside the battleship.

Everyone knows now that before the day is done *Yamato* will have done her duty to Emperor and to destiny, for better or for worse, and a solemn sense of camaraderie unites the three thousand – admirals to ratings, bridge to engine-room. By noon Admiral Ito, the force commander,

Opposite: Yamato *(right) and four of her escort ships zig-zagging in formation,* April 7, 1945

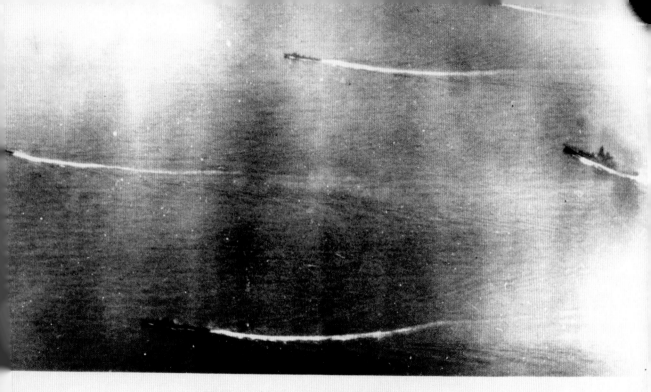

TASK GROUP BEFORE ATTACK

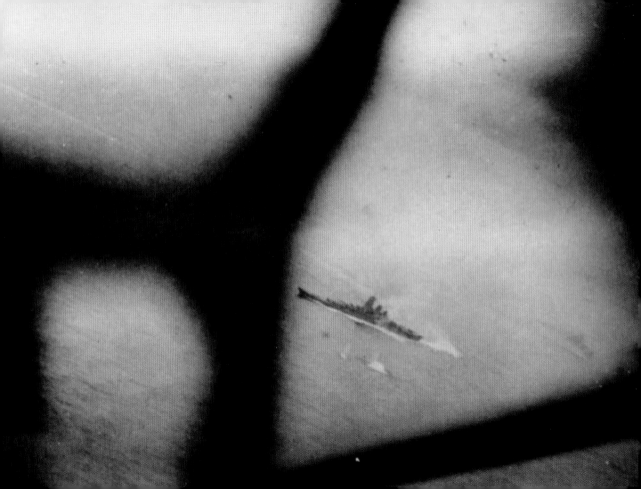

is seated in his chair on the combat bridge, immobile, unsmiling, arms folded, ready for battle: and at 1220 the radar room reports that three large formations of enemy aircraft are approaching from the south. Ten minutes later Chaos strikes.

★ ★ ★

It takes three and a half hours to sink the battleship, and throughout the battle Admiral Ito is silent on that bridge, while *Yamato* sails on at 24 knots, and her consorts race around her. And out of the skies, in three violent waves in as many hours, 386 American aircraft fall upon the Task Force in deafening fury, swooping to the attack almost at sea-level, instantly racing off and leaving behind them, one after the other, endless explosions of water and debris. The air is thick with projectiles, torpedoes flying through the air or scudding across the sea, rockets and bombs and a myriad bullets. Sardonically bright colours are everywhere – the crimson

Opposite: Yamato *turns sharply to avoid a torpedo and a bomb, seen from an attacking Helldiver*

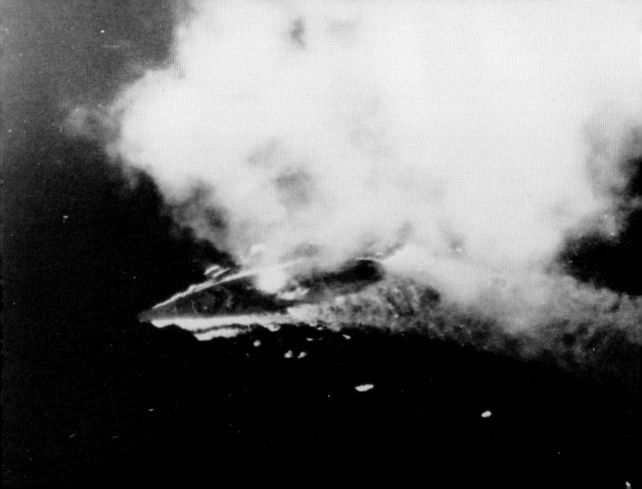

Previous pages: Yamato *manoeuvering evasively at a brisk 15-20 knots during the first attack; a fire can already be seen but there is as yet no list*

During the second attack: Yamato *is struggling; she is down at the bow, and moving slowly. The destroyer, either* Fuyuzuki *or* Suzutsuki, *has just fired her 100 mm guns towards the attacking planes, including the one from which this photograph was taken*

Manoeuvering becomes more frantic as **Yamato** *is pounded relentlessly. The plane on the right is a Curtiss Helldiver*

flashes of guns and shell-bursts, the paintwork of the screaming aircraft, the white and yellow streaks of tracer bullets, and half-hidden by smoke at *Yamato*'s mast-head, the three fluttering flags, red, white and black, of the battleship's pre-eminence.

And every man does his duty. The noise is deafening, and through it all, unmistakable among the bomb explosions and the machine-gun chatter and the howls of the strafing, swarming aircraft, there repeatedly sound the deep tremendous roars of *Yamato*'s 18-inch guns, contributing those Beehive shells to the frenzy. The battleship never gives up, never stops firing, never lowers its flags, but its defiance makes no difference anyway. It is as though some grand beast, the tiger unleashed, is tormented by insufferable insects in hopeless conflict: and Admiral Ito sits there passionless in his chair as one by one the ships of his fleet are sunk or disabled around him; until at last, after three hours of it, repeatedly shattered by bombs and torpedoes but with her guns always blazing, her flags still flying, with a mighty shudder *Yamato* herself begins to heel over, and slowly capsizes.

Opposite: A bomb explodes on Yamato*'s port side. The near misses caused even more damage than the direct hits*

Yamato *very near
the end. She is down
at the bow and listing
heavily to port; fire is
raging amidships*

Over the loudhailers the order comes to abandon ship, and Ito impassively leaves his chair and locks himself in his cabin to die. At 1345 hours a gigantic explosion sends the battleship to the bottom of the Pacific, together with Ito, Ariga and 2,278 of the men under their command.

Only a handful of American fliers have died in the action, only a few aircraft have been shot down, and for me everything about the story now becomes cruelly figurative, even to the types of the American aircraft that won the fight – Hellcats, Helldivers, Corsairs, Avengers and Wildcats . . .

Picasso foresaw it all, on our behalf. He saw the explicit pattern of it, the completeness. The agony is there of course, in the picture's grieving women and wounded animals, and anger, and pity, and disenchantment: but there is at least the beauty of hope, too, in the unlit lamp of peace, and even perhaps a touch of irony – for if there is something absolute in

Opposite: "A red ball of flame" – Yamato *at the moment of the final explosion*

Smoke billows up from underwater explosions as Yamato *sinks. The other three ships are the remains of her escort*

the composition, Picasso knew, as Kipling knew, and as we know better than either, that there is no discharge in the wars . . .

The tremendous column of black smoke that rose from the sea at the site of *Yamato*'s sinking could be seen from the shores of Japan itself, where the cherry trees blossomed.

★ ★ ★

Years later Admiral Samuel Eliot Morison, the official historian of the US Navy, wrote that the sinking of *Yamato* had "a sentimental interest for all sailors – when she went down, five centuries of naval warfare ended." There were much greater meanings to the event, though. It symbolized not just the end of the battleship era, but the end of *Banzai* and all that, perhaps even the end of the imperial idea itself, the world over. It was one of history's disillusionments.

Two months later, sure enough, the Americans dropped their nuclear bombs on Nagasaki and Hiroshima and invaded the Japanese mainland, clinching their victory. The Imperial Japanese Navy was dissolved at once, and became the Japan Maritime Self-Defence Force, but it was another six years before the Japanese Empire made peace with the United States and with forty-eight other allied nations, in the San Francisco Treaty of 1951 – the closing of a chapter in the history of man, declared the Prime Minister of Ceylon, and the beginning of a new one...

Thus it took a statesman from a far, far lesser Power, a Power that never had a battleship, to articulate the last of war's ironic beauties – the lovely peace, that is, of reconciliation.

Valedictory

So if there is much misery to Yamato's *story, there is beauty too – a terrible beauty, as the Irish poet Yeats had written of another conflict not long before.*

I think a proper music to orchestrate the end of the tale is neither discordant nor tragic, but, like Beethoven's Ode to Joy, at once somehow grand, pathetic and grateful. Nobody ever built another Yamato. *The Japanese themselves had begun one, but it was converted into an aircraft carrier when the truths of contemporary sea-warfare became clear, and inevitably it was also sunk by the Americans before the war was done.* Yamato *herself lived on, though, in legend and in folk-memory. Not for years after the war was everything known to the world about her weaponry and armour, but films were made about her, books were written, tales were told, and a spectral descendant, Space Battleship Yamato, entered the Japanese national consciousness as a figure of graphic art in an animated strip – recognizably related to the original, but equipped with wings, jets and, of course, nuclear weapons.*

The passing of the generations gave to the story of the ship an extra pride, loyalty and regret. When in 1985 her remains were identified at the bottom of the Pacific, it was decided not to raise them, but to leave them in magnanimous memorial. And do we not share that instinct, you and I, as we read of her fate? Her cause was crazy and cruel, but her conduct was honourable, and the fact that those 2,278 Japanese men, admirals to deckhands, fought to the death in such style for such unnecessary reasons in such momentous allegory makes her end, to my mind, all the more touching.

So the last picture I have chosen to illustrate our narrative is not one of despair, tragedy or defiance in defeat, but one that displays a more consolatory aspect of war. It is Diego Velázquez's Surrender of Breda, *painted in 1634, which shows a Dutch commander surrendering the city to his victorious Spanish opponent in a conflict of those times. The Spanish commander was actually a Genoese, the Dutch soon recovered and won the war, but anyway there is no dazzle of triumph in this picture, and no shame of failure either*

    The armies confront each other still cap-à-pie beneath a forest of lances, but the two commanders meet courteously, like friends or comrades: and the

Opposite: The Surrender of Breda, *by Diego Velázquez, 1634*

BATTLESHIP YAMATO

message of the painting, as moving today as it was when it was painted four centuries ago, is one of kindness – which is, to my mind, the truest concomitant of beauty, the prime antidote to the madness of war, and so proper, I suggest, to the memory of IJN Yamato, launched 1940 at Kure, sunk 180 miles south-west of Kyushu, April 7, 1945.

Thanks

My son Mark, in Canada, has helped me with his thoughts about the temper and allusions of this project, and I offer it with love and gratitude to him and his siblings, Henry, Twm and Suki.

Among the scores of books that have memorialized *Yamato,* three pioneers of the genre in particular have been essential reading for me, and will be invaluable to anyone wanting harder truth about the end of the battleship: *The Two-Ocean War,* by Samuel Eliot Morison (1963), *A Glorious Way to Die,* by Russell Spurr (1982), and *Requiem for Battleship* Yamato, by Yoshida Mitsuru (translated by Richard Minear, 1985).

At the Yamato Museum in Kure there is an immaculate 1:10 scale model of *Yamato,* and standing beside it is as close as you or I could ever get to the presence of such an ironically beautiful instrument of death.

Trefan Morys, 2017

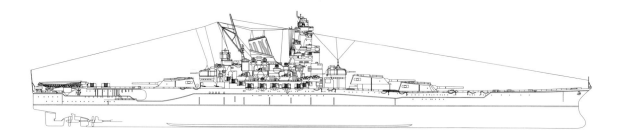

IJN *Yamato*

Length: 862 feet 10 inches (263 m)
Beam: 121 feet 1 inch (36.9 m)
Draught: 32 feet 11 inches (10.03 m)
Speed: 27.7 knots on trials
Launched: August 8, 1940
Completed: December 16, 1941
Deemed operational: May 27, 1942. Fleet flagship
Sunk: April 7, 1945

No. 1 Alert Cruising Formation

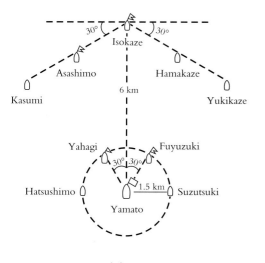

No. 3 Alert Cruising Formation

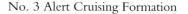

Distance
= 1,500 m

大和　Yamato ('Great Harmony')
矢矧　Yahagi (from the River Yahagi)
磯風　Isokaze ('Wind on the Beach')
浜風　Hamakaze ('Beach Wind')
雪風　Yukikaze ('Snowy Wind')

冬月　Fuyuzuki ('Winter Moon')
涼月　Suzutsuki ('Clear Moon in Autumn')
初霜　Hatsushimo ('First Frost')
霞　　Kasumi ('Haze')
朝霜　Asashimo ('Morning Frost')

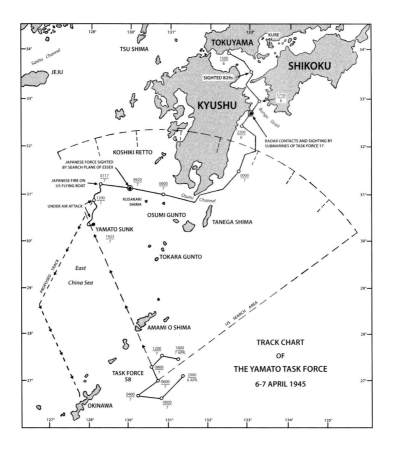

TRACK CHART

OF

THE YAMATO TASK FORCE

6-7 APRIL 1945

Yamato Action – April 5-7, 1945

5 April:

1500   Received Combined Fleet DesOpOrd No. 607.

6 April:

1520   1st Diversion Attack Force (*Yamato*, *Yahagi*), DesDiv 41 (*Fuyutsuki*, *Suzutsuki*), DesDiv 17 (*Isokaze*, *Hamakaze*, *Yukikaze*), DesDiv 21 (*Asashimo*, *Hatsushimo*, *Kasumi*) sorties from off Tokuyama.

1710   Float reconnaissance plane of Saeki Air Group detects what seems to be an enemy submarine.

2000   Negotiate Bungo Channel. Change to course 140° at point bearing 140° distance 2.5 miles from southern tip of Fukashima. Assume No. 1 alert cruising disposition. Speed 22 knots, pursuing simultaneous zigzag manoeuvre, 'i' time interval method.

7 April:

0300   Negotiated Osumi Channel, assuming No. 1 alert cruising disposition. Course, 220°; speed 22 knots; simultaneous zigzag manoeuvre, 'i' time interval method.

0345   Changed course to 280° at point bearing 193° distance 8 miles from Sata Misaki.

0600   Assume No. 3 Alert Cruising Disposition.

0840   Note 5 enemy carrier-based planes at point bearing 150° distance 40 km.

1014   Note that 2 enemy flying boats have contacted the 1st Diversion Attack Force at point bearing 230° distance 45 km.

1016   Simultaneous turn to right to 180°.

1017   Commence firing main and auxiliary batteries at flying boats noted above.

1018   Cease firing. Lose above planes in clouds.

1020   Simultaneous turn to 230°.

1045   Simultaneous turn to 160°. Speed 20 knots.

1057   Simultaneous turn to 210°.

1110   Sight contacting plane bearing 180° distance 5 km. Make simultaneous turn to 240°. Speed 24 knots.

1119   Turn to 270°.

1125   Turn to 240°.

1129   Turn to 205° and head for scheduled course.

1133   Speed 22 knots.

1135   Sight 7 enemy carried-based planes bearing 270° distance 40 km.

1141   Simultaneous turn to 180°.

1145   Resume zigzagging.

1222   Note the Oshima Transportation Unit bearing 250° distance 45 km.

1232   Note 150 enemy carrier-based planes bearing 130° distance 50 km.

1234   Speed 24 knots. Cease zigzagging. Commence firing at the aircraft noted above.

1237   Independent evasive manoeuvres to port. Course, 100°.

1240   All units pursue 100° course. Several SB2Cs commence diving bearing 90°.

1240   One shot down.

1241   Evasive manoeuvres independently at maximum battle speed. Two medium-sized bombs hit near aft mast. Aft fire control room, No. 2 auxiliary gun, No. 13 radar damaged.

1243   5 torpedo planes head for ship from point bearing 70° to port, distance 7,000 metres. Undertake to evade independently.

1243   3 torpedo tracks noted at point bearing 90° to port, distance 1,000 metres.

1245   One torpedo hit in port-forward.

1257   Several SB2Cs go into dive from starboard-stern. One shot down.

1300   Set course on 180°.

1302   New target of 50 planes sighted bearing 200° distance 30 km.

1322   Simultaneous turn to starboard to 210°.

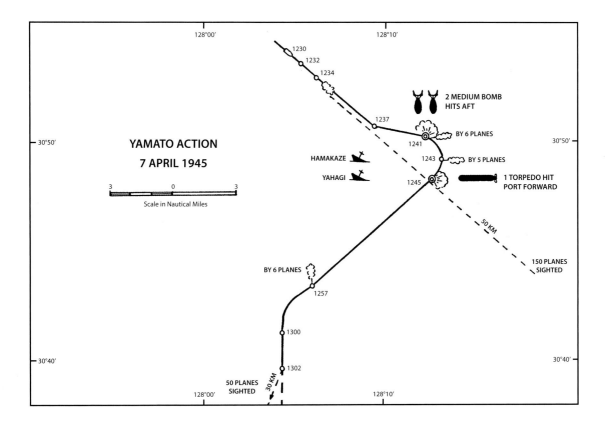

YAMATO ACTION

7 APRIL 1945

Scale in Nautical Miles

3   0   3

128°00' 128°10'

30°50'

1230
1232
1234

1237

2 MEDIUM BOMB
HITS AFT

1241   BY 6 PLANES

HAMAKAZE

YAHAGI

1243   BY 5 PLANES

1245   1 TORPEDO HIT
PORT FORWARD

30°50'

50 KM

150 PLANES
SIGHTED

BY 6 PLANES

1257

1300

1302

30°40'

30°40'

50 PLANES
SIGHTED

30 KM

128°00' 128°10'

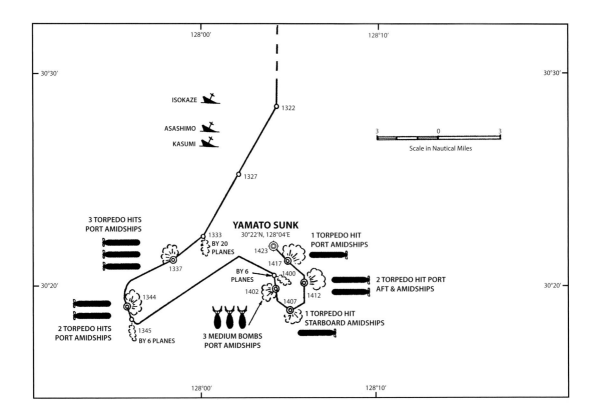

ISOKAZE

ASASHIMO

KASUMI

1322

1327

3 TORPEDO HITS
PORT AMIDSHIPS

1333
BY 20
PLANES

1337

YAMATO SUNK
30°22'N, 128°04'E

1423

1417

1400

BY 6
PLANES

1402

1407

1412

1344

1345
BY 6 PLANES

2 TORPEDO HITS
PORT AMIDSHIPS

3 MEDIUM BOMBS
PORT AMIDSHIPS

1 TORPEDO HIT
PORT AMIDSHIPS

2 TORPEDO HIT PORT
AFT & AMIDSHIPS

1 TORPEDO HIT
STARBOARD AMIDSHIPS

128°00'

128°10'

30°30'

30°30'

30°20'

30°20'

3   0   3

Scale in Nautical Miles

128°00'

128°10'

1327   Speed 22 knots.

1333   20 torpedo planes head for ship from point bearing 60° to port distance 4,000 metres.

1334   Note 6 torpedo tracks bearing 50° to port distance 2,000 metres.

1337   3 torpedo hits port amidship. Auxiliary steering gear is damaged.

1340   Simultaneous turn to starboard to 230°.

1341   Note 4 torpedo tracks bearing 60° distance 7,000 metres.

1342   Attempt independent evasive manoeuvres. 1 torpedo plane shot down 500 metres from bow.

1344   2 torpedo hits port amidship.

1345   Fix auxiliary steering gear at centre position and change course to 205°. Several SB2Cs dive on ship from bow. Attempt evasion. 2 SB2Cs shot down.

1400   Several SB2Cs dive on ship from starboard-bow.

1402   3 medium-type bomb hits port amidship.

1405   Note 1 torpedo track bearing 60° to starboard distance 800 metres.

1407   1 torpedo hit on starboard amidship.

1410   Note 4 torpedo tracks bearing 60° to port, distance 1,000 metres.

1412   2 torpedo hits on portside, amidship and aft. Set course on 0°. Actual speed 12 knots. Listing to port 6°.

1415   Note 1 torpedo track bearing 90° to port distance 1,000 metres.

1417   1 torpedo hit on portside amidship. Angle of list increasing rapidly.

1420   Listing to port 20°.

1423   Induced explosion blows up forward and aft turrets resulting in ship's sinking.

Results obtained:

   Shot down 5 planes   Damaged 20 planes

Damages suffered:

   Sunk (killed in action, including Captain) 2,498

Picture credits

pp. 2–3: *Yamato* during running trials, Sukumo Bay, October 30, 1941. Photograph Yamato Museum, Kure

pp. 4–5 *The hero Coxinga faces a tiger,* triptych woodblock print by Utagawa Kuniyoshi, *c.* 1842. The hero Coxinga, fighting for the Qing in Korea, confronts a tiger who has killed one of his men

p. 6: Wooden construction model of *Yamato*, date uncertain. Photograph Yamato Museum, Kure

p. 9: HMS *Prince of Wales*, Singapore, 1941. Later that year she was the first battleship to be sunk by airpower

p. 10: *Bismarck* in 1940. US Naval History and Heritage Command photograph

pp. 12–13: *Yamato* performing full power trials, Sukumo Bay, October 30, 1941. Photograph Yamato Museum, Kure

p. 14: *Yamato* at anchor, 1942 or 1943. Japanese Nakajima B5N2 torpedo bombers (Allied classification "Kate") fly overhead. These planes were used in the attack on Pearl Harbor. Photograph Yamato Museum, Kure

p. 16: Attic black–figure neck amphora, near Medea Group, *c.* 510 BC (detail). Los Angeles, J. Paul Getty Museum

p. 17: P/O Kenneth "Hawkeye" Lee at the centre of a mixed group of British, Commonwealth and Polish airmen at RAF Hawkinge, July 1940. Ministry of Information photograph

pp. 18–19: *Léonidas aux Thermopyles* (detail), by Jacques-Louis David, 1814. Paris, Louvre

p. 21: *Tirpitz* in the Altafjord, winter 1943

p. 22: *Yamato* at the Truk anchorage, Caroline Islands, where she spent much of 1943. US Naval History and Heritage Command photograph

pp. 24–25: *Yamato* in action during the Battle off Samar, October 25, 1944. Photographed from a USS *Petrof Bay* (CVE-80) plane. US Naval History and Heritage Command photograph

p. 26: *Yamato* (or *Musashi*), with the chrysanthemum crest just visible on a ship in the foreground, 1943. Photograph Yamato Museum, Kure

p. 27: The Emperor visits *Musashi* in Yokosuka Naval Arsenal, June 24, 1943. Photograph Yamato Museum, Kure

p. 28: The Emperor inspects equipment on the upper bridge of *Musashi,* June 24,1943. Photograph Yamato Museum, Kure

p. 30: *Yamato* retreating from the Battle of the Sibuyan Sea, October 26, 1944. Photograph taken from a B-24 Liberator. US Naval History and Heritage Command photograph

p. 34: Sailors relaxing on the foredeck of *Musashi* during trials in June–July 1942, Inland Sea. The uncluttered deck would later be covered with anti-aircraft 25 mm guns. Photograph Yamato Museum, Kure

p. 37: Navigation Department Cadets (4th Grade) aboard *Yamato* March 1945. Photograph Yamato Museum, Kure

p. 38: Promotion ceremony aboard *Yamato*, March 1945. Photograph Yamato Museum, Kure

pp. 40–41: *Blossoming Cherry Trees,* 1805, by Sakai Hoitsu (1761–1828). Pair of six-leaf screens: principal part of left screen and part of right screen. New York, Metropolitan Museum of Art. Photograph courtesy MMA

p. 42: *Yamato,* seen from the stern, in the last stages of fitting out in the shipyard, Kure, September 20, 1941. The aircraft carrier *Hosho* is at the extreme right. The store ship *Mamiya* is in the centre distance. *Yamato*'s after 460 mm (18.1-inch) main battery gun turret is seen with one barrel at maximum elevation, and above is the superfiring 155 mm secondary battery gun turret. Photograph Yamato Museum, Kure

p. 45: Part of the revolving structure of the colossal 18.1-inch triple gun turrets of *Yamato* being assembled, June 3, 1940. Photograph Yamato Museum, Kure

p. 47: *Yamato* manoeuvering to avoid aerial attack, October 24, 1944. The shadow of an American plane can be seen. US Naval History and Heritage Command photograph

p. 48: Rear-Admiral Ariga Kosaku

p. 49: Anti-aircraft gunners – Group 12 of the 25 mm guns aboard *Yamato*, 1945. Photograph Yamato Museum, Kure

p. 50: Warrant officers photographed aboard *Yamato*, January 1945. Photograph Yamato Museum, Kure

p 53: USS *Yorktown* (CV-10): view looking aft on the flight deck, in November–December 1943, at the time of the Marshalls–Gilberts Operation. Planes are F6Fs, TBMs, and SBDs. Photograph by Kerlee. US Naval History and Heritage Command photograph

p. 54: Admiral Ryunosuke Kusaka. One of the main planners of the attack on Pearl Harbor, Kusaka was also a noted swordsman

pp. 56-57: *Campagne de France, 1814* (detail), by Ernest Meissonier, 1864. Paris, Musée d'Orsay

p. 58: The Japanese Center Force leaves Brunei Bay, Borneo, October 22, 1944, en route to the Philippines. Ships are, from right to left: battleships *Nagato*, *Musashi* and *Yamato*; heavy cruisers *Maya*, *Chokai*, *Takao*, *Atago*, *Haguro* and *Myoko*. Courtesy of Lieutenant Tobei Shiraishi. US Naval History and Heritage Command photograph

pp. 60–61: *Washington Crossing the Delaware* (detail), 1851, by Emanuel Leutze. New York, Metropolitan Museum of Art. Photograph courtesy MMA

p. 62: The 18.1-inch "Beehive" shells designed for *Yamato*, on display at Willard Park, Washington Naval Yard, DC in 1975. U.S. Naval History and Heritage Command photograph

p. 63: Helldiver bombers with ships of Task Force 58 on their way to Kyushu, March 1945, US Naval History and Heritage Command photograph

p. 64: Admiral Raymond A. Spruance, USN and Vice Admiral Marc A. Mitscher, USN at a Staff Conference at Saipan, Marianas Islands. US Naval History and Heritage Command photograph

p. 66: Vice-Admiral Seiichi Ito on *Yamato*. January 1945. Photograph Yamato Museum, Kure

pp. 68–69 and 70: *Guernica* by Pablo Picasso (detail and complete painting) 1937, Madrid, Musee Reina Sofia. © Succession Picasso/DACS London 2017

p. 73: *Yamato* zig-zagging in formation with four destroyers. Photographed by a plane from USS *Bennington* just before the first attack at 12.30; from the *Bennington* action report. US Naval History and Heritage Command photograph courtesy of US Naval Academy

p. 74: *Yamato* turning sharply during second attack by planes from USS *Essex*. The two splashes are a torpedo (left) and bomb (right). Photograph taken by rear gunner of a Curtiss SB2C Helldiver. US Naval History and Heritage Command photograph courtesy of US Naval Academy

pp. 76–77: Original caption: "The 72,000-ton Japanese battleship *Yamato*, pride of the Imperial Fleet, maneuvers evasively at a brisk 15 to 20 knots prior to attack. One fire can be observed amidships from previous attacks, but at this point no list has developed. Photographed from a USS *Yorktown* (CV-10) plane." US Naval History and Heritage Command photograph

pp. 78–79: From original caption: "*Yamato* seen after multiple air attacks with one of her escort destroyers, either

Fuyuzuki or *Suzutsuki*. She is down at the bow and moving slowly." US Naval History and Heritage Command photograph

pp. 80–81: *Yamato* under attack by Curtiss SB2C Helldivers, one of which is seen to the right. Photograph Historical/Corbis Historical/Getty Images

p. 82: From original caption: "*Yamato* manoeuvres frantically under attack as a bomb explodes off its port side. [The speed with which *Yamato* was sunk owed much to the concentration of the attack on one side.] The fire in the area of the 6.1 inch turret can be clearly seen." US Naval History and Heritage Command photograph

pp. 84–85: From original caption: "Japanese battleship *Yamato* lists to port just prior to VT-9 (USS *Yorktown*) torpedo attack. She is making 10-15 knots. Photographed from a USS *Yorktown* (CV-10) plane." US Naval History and Heritage Command photograph

p. 87: Original caption: "A split-second shot of *Yamato* as she blew up. A red ball of flame envelops this mightiest of Japanese battleships, and a moment later it shoots like a comet to the clouds, 2,000 feet high. Photographed from a USS *Yorktown* (CV-10) plane." US Naval History and

Heritage Command photograph

pp. 88–89: From original caption: "Japanese battleship *Yamato* blows up after receiving massive bomb and torpedo damage from U.S. Navy carrier planes, north of Okinawa on 7 April 1945. Three Japanese destroyers are nearby." US Naval History and Heritage Command photograph

p. 92: The bow of *Yamato* photographed October 2016. Photograph Yamato Museum, Kure

pp. 95 and 97: *The Surrender at Breda,* Diego Velázquez, 1634. Madrid, Museo del Prado

p. 98: Wooden construction model of *Yamato*, date uncertain. Photograph Yamato Museum, Kure

p. 100: Elevation of *Yamato* by www.the-blueprints.com

p. 101: Alert Formation Nos. 1 and 3, adapted by Patrick Davies from volume 56 of *Senshi Sosho,* Tokyo, 1966-1980

pp. 102, 105 and 106: Maps of *Yamato* sortie and action, adapted by Patrick Davies from US Strategic Bombing Survey (Pacific), *The Campaigns of the Pacific War,* Washington, 1946

With special thanks to Rei Kozaki and the Yamato Museum, Kure; to the US Naval History and Heritage Command; and to Anaïs Métais and Patrick Davies

For information about special discounts for bulk purchases, please contact: W. W. Norton Special Sales at
specialsales@wwnorton.com or 800-233-4830

Book design by Pallas Athene: Alexander Fyjis-Walker with Patrick Davies and Anaïs Métais

Library of Congress Cataloging-in-Publication Data

Names: Morris, Jan, 1926– author.
Title: Battleship Yamato : of war, beauty and irony / Jan Morris.
Description: First American edition. | New York : Liveright Publishing Corporation, [2017]
Identifiers: LCCN 2017035438 | ISBN 9781631493423 (hardcover)
Subjects: LCSH: Yamato (Battleship) | World War, 1939–1945—Naval operations, Japanese.
Classification: LCC D777.5.Y33 M67 2017 | DDC 940.54/5952—dc23
LC record available at https://lccn.loc.gov/2017035438

Liveright Publishing Corporation, 500 Fifth Avenue, New York, NY 10110
www.wwnorton.com

W. W. Norton & Company Ltd., 15 Carlisle Street, London W1D 3BS

1 2 3 4 5 6 7 8 9 0